Trea
Spir

THE FRUITS OF
THE SPIRIT
by
EVELYN UNDERHILL

Compiled by
Roger L. Roberts

MOREHOUSE PUBLISHING

First USA edition published 1982
Morehouse Publishing
P.O. Box 1321
Harrisburg, PA 17105

Third Printing, 1995

Printed in the United States of America

PREFACE

THE PAGES which follow have been extracted
from a book, *The Fruits of the Spirit*, which
was first published (together with a few letters
of spiritual counsel) in 1942, the year after the
death of its distinguished author, Evelyn
Underhill.

The book was modestly described by her
husband, in his introduction to the first edition, as something which he knew that its
author would not have claimed as in any sense
a literary work, since it merely consisted of
a series of informal addresses given to a small
group of like-minded people and intended
rather to stimulate meditation than to give
information. However, it affords a brilliant
example of Evelyn Underhill's gift for com-
bining an insight into the heights and depths

of Christian spiritual experience with a down-to-earth appreciation of the actual circumstances in which modern Christians are called to walk the Christian way. This is certainly a book, with its vivid sense of the reality of the Eternal and with a no less vivid (and sometimes humorous) awareness of the practicalities of daily life, which offers inspired guidance to anyone desiring to bring forth the fruits of the Spirit in the world of time.

The author was a notable scholar, widely recognised in her day as one of the leading English authorities on Christian mysticism. Her academic distinction is evident in these pages. But what matters much more, the reader will find here an author whose own passionate but disciplined devotional practice enabled her with moving simplicity to point others to the way of the Cross in the power of the Spirit.

R.L.R.

ALONE WITH GOD

WE ALL know pretty well why we come into Retreat: we come to seek the opportunity of being alone with God and attending to God, in order that we may do His will better in our everyday lives. We have come to live for a few days the life of prayer and deepen our contact with the spiritual realities on which our lives depend—to recover if we can our spiritual poise. We do not come for spiritual information, but for spiritual food and air— to wait on the Lord and renew our strength— not for our own sakes but for the sake of the world.

Now Christ, who so seldom gave detailed instruction about anything, did give some detailed instruction for that withdrawal, that recollection which is the essential condition of real prayer, real communion with God.

'Thou when thou prayest, enter into thy closet—and *shut the door.*' I think we can almost see the smile with which He said those

three words: and those three words define
what we have to try to do. Anyone can retire
into a quiet place and have a thoroughly un-
quiet time in it—but that is not making a
Retreat! It is the shutting of the door which
makes the whole difference between a true
Retreat and a worried religious weekend.

Shut the door. It is an extraordinary difficult thing to do. Nearly every one pulls it to
and leaves it slightly ajar so that a whistling
draught comes in from the outer world, with
reminders of all the worries, interests, con-
flicts, joys and sorrows of daily life.

But Christ said Shut, and He meant Shut.
A complete barrier deliberately set up, with
you on one side alone with God and everything else without exception on the other side.
The voice of God is very gentle; we cannot
hear it if we let other voices compete. Our
ordinary life, of course, is not lived like that
and should not be; but this bit of life is to be
lived like that. It is no use at all to enter that
closet, that inner sanctuary, clutching the

daily paper, the reports of all the societies you support, your engagement book and a large bundle of personal correspondence. All these must be left outside. The motto for your Retreat is *God Only*, God in Himself, sought for Himself alone.

The object of Retreat is not Intercession or self exploration, but such communion with Him as shall afterwards make you more powerful in intercession; and such self-loss in Him as shall heal your wounds by new contact with His life and love.

You would hardly enter the presence of the human being you most deeply respected and loved in the state of fuss and preoccupation and distraction in which we too often approach God. You are to 'centre down' as the Quakers say, into that deep stillness which is the proper atmosphere of your soul. Remain with God. Wait upon the Light. Speak to your heavenly Father who is in secret. These are the words that describe the attitude of the soul really in Retreat. Do not think now of the world's state and needs and sufferings or of your problems and responsibilities; this is not the time for that. Do not think too much about your own sins. A general, humble, but very tranquil act of penitence and acknowledgement of your faultiness is best. 'Commune with your Father, which is in secret.' There is always something dark, hidden, secret, about our real intercourse with God. In religion we should always distrust the obvious and the clear. The closet where we speak to Him is not very well lit—but the light that filters into it has a quality of its own; it is a ray of the Eternal Light on which we cannot easily look: but as we get used to it, sun ourselves in its glow, we learn, as we can bear it, to see more and more. Therefore we must be content to dwell with God in that dim silence. Gaze at Him *darkly*, as the mystics say, offer yourselves again and again to Him. 'All Friends everywhere,' said Fox, 'keep all your meetings, *waiting* on the Light'—a perfect prescription for a good Retreat.

The Fruits of the Spirit: Evelyn Underhill

The Light, Life and Love of God—which are all the same thing really—are aspects of His Being, His Living Presence, and will be disclosed in the silence to each soul according to its capacity and need. Let us try to see our situation in that large and general way: our small imperfect little souls, waiting here on the Eternal God, already fully present in His splendour; and His living Spirit, which is His Love, gradually penetrating and fertilizing all our lives; reaching into and transforming the most humble activities of those lives, making them what God wants them to be.

When we shut the door, we did not shut any part of ourselves away from God—not even the most irreligious bits. Wait with much confidence. He may take as fuel for the fire upon His altar, the most unexpected bit—something we had never thought of in connection with our spiritual lives. So let us offer *all* that we have and are and give thanks.

'Remember,' said the Abbé de Rourville, 'that God loves your soul, not in some aloof, impersonal way, but passionately, with the adoring, cherishing love of a parent for a child. The outpouring of His Holy Spirit is really the outpouring of His love, surrounding and penetrating your little soul with a peaceful, joyful delight in His creature: tolerant, peaceful, a love full of long-suffering and gentleness, working quietly, able to wait for results, faithful, devoted, without variableness or shadow of turning. Such is the charity of God.'

BRINGING FORTH FRUIT

We too easily think of the gift of the Spirit as something administered to us or inserted in us—perhaps a little supernatural seed planted in the soul—'Receive the Holy Spirit.' But it is God Himself in His Reality (not some gift or faculty, some new element) Who comes again and again in His creative power into the heart of our life. 'Receive the Holy Spirit' means 'Receive *God*.' The stress for us lies not on His ceaseless giving but on our *receiving*. He, as St. John of the Cross says, does not change, but we do. His pressure on our souls is constant. Our self-opening to that pressure is part of our freedom and becomes fuller, deeper, more generous with the growth of our prayer: and the more entirely that Spirit, that Life of God possesses us, the more fully and inevitably it will bring forth its fruits. The Holy Spirit is the Spirit of Creation and where He is present there is always growth, never sterility.

So the reality, the living quality of our prayer, our communion with God, can best be tested by the gradual growth in us of these fruits of Divine Love; and it is of those we are specially to think. They are real fruits and therefore they grow by their inherent vitality, at their own pace, hardly observed till they are ripe. They are not something we can model with deliberate effort in spiritual plasticine. Perhaps you think you have only produced a few small green apples—wait patiently till the sunshine of God brings them to maturity.

'The fruit of the Spirit,' says St. Paul, 'is Love, Joy, Peace, Long-suffering, Gentleness, Goodness, Faithfulness, Meekness, Temperance'—all the things the world most needs. A clear issue, is it not? To discover the health and reality of our life of prayer, we need not analyse it or fuss about it. But we must consider whether it tends, or does not tend, to produce just these fruits, because they are the necessary results of the action of God in the soul. These are the fruits of human nature when it has opened itself to the action of the Eternal Love: what the 'new creature in Christ' (which if we are really Christians, we are all in process of becoming) is to be like. So they are very good subjects for meditation. A good gardener always has an idea of what he is trying to grow; without vision even a cabbage patch will perish.

Now don't let us think of the Fruits of the Spirit as if they were religious counterparts of

those plump, outsize specimens with a sus-
piciously polished surface, which we see laid
out at the village flower show. We are not to
expect anything striking like that, or rove
round our internal premises anxiously looking
to see how our Joy and Peace are getting on
and putting them in muslin bags to keep off
the wasps. Here we are confronted by something far greater, deeper and more mysterious
than the individual quality of individual souls.
The Fruits of the Spirit are those dispositions,
those ways of thinking, speaking and acting,
which are brought forth in us, gradually but
inevitably, by the pressure of the Divine Love
in our souls. They all spring from that one
root.

We might call them manifestations of the
Mind of God in His Creation; manifestations
of His unlimited and generous love, His essential joy, His deep tranquillity, the un-
marred harmony of His nature, His patient,
gentle action, His faithful and cherishing care.
The very meaning of Christianity is the trans-

figuration of Creation by making it the expression of God's Word and Spirit. And in us too—members of Christ and children of the Eternal Perfect—this, if we are docile and self-emptied, will be done. For we are part of a world that is being made, a world that shall manifest in visible form the perfection and beauty of God.

I do not think that St. Paul arranged his list of the fruits of the Spirit in a casual order. They represent a progressive series from one point and that one point is Love, the living eternal seed from which all grow. We all know that Christians are baptized 'into a life summed up in love,' even though we have to spend the rest of our own lives learning how to do it. Love therefore is the budding point from which all the rest come: that tender, cherishing attitude; that unlimited self-forgetfulness, generosity and kindness which is the attitude of God to all His creatures and so must be the attitude towards them which His Spirit brings forth in us. If that is frostbitten we need not hope for any of the rest. 'Who so dwelleth in Charity dwelleth in God and God in him.' To be unloving is to be out of touch with God. So the generous, cherishing, Divine love, the indiscriminate delight in others, just and unjust, must be our model too. Be ye perfect. To come down to brass tacks, God loves the horrid man at the fish-shop, and the tiresome woman in the next flat, and the disappointing Vicar, and the mulish parent, and the contractor who has cut down the row of trees we loved to build a lot of revolting bungalows. God *loves*, not tolerates, these wayward, half-grown, self-centred spirits and seeks without ceasing to draw them into His love. And the first-fruit of His indwelling presence, the first sign that we are on His side and He on ours, must be at least a tiny bud of this Charity breaking the hard and rigid outline of our life.

THE PEACE OF GOD

Peace is a word that echoes through the New Testament, nearly always coupled with the idea of a disclosure of truth which adjusts us to life: something which annuls self-interest, anxiety and fear, transcending the apparent injustice and cruelty of life and harmonizing our fugitive experience with the all-encompassing will of God.

On earth peace . . .

Lord, now lettest Thou Thy servant depart in peace . . .

My peace I give unto you, My peace I leave with you . . .

And He stood among them and said, Peace be unto you . . .

The peace of the Lord be always with you . . .

Take any one of these texts and replace it in its New Testament setting among the dangers, uncertainties and sufferings of the early

Christians, and see what it has to say to your soul. Consider that it was not during His ministry in Galilee, but when He drew near the crisis and agony of the Passion and the tension of His own life was great, that Christ more and more emphasized peace. 'Peace I give unto you, not as the world giveth give I unto you'—I give the deep, enduring, tranquil peace, the inward quiet of acceptance, the mind stayed on God ready for anything because anchored on His Eternal Reality—indifferent to its own risks, comforts or achievements, sunk in the great movement of His life.

That sounds all right and sometimes in prayer we seem to draw near it; but the test comes later on, when this peace and joy must be matched against the troubles and assaults, the evils, cruelties and contradictions of the world. Then we shall see whether our peace is just a feeling or a fact—a true *fruit* which exists and endures, grows and ripens in the sun and wind of experience. For the peace of

God does not mean apathy in respect of the world's sorrows and sins. It can co-exist with the sharpest pain, the utmost bewilderment, the agony of compassion which feels the whole awful weight of evil and suffering. We see this so clearly in the Saints who bore the whole weight of redemptive suffering with a tranquil joy—for this peace of God is linked with the Altar and the Cross.

'O Lamb of God, that takest away the sins of the world, grant us Thy peace!' That is a tremendous prayer to take on our lips, for it means peace at a great price; the peace of the Cross, of absolute acceptance, utter abandonment to God—a peace inseparable from sacrifice. The peace-offering, you remember, was one of the three great Temple sacrifices and the one in which the offerer drew nearest to God and had communion with God.

Just consider in this respect the end of the Gospel of St. Luke: when those who had been nearest Christ, who loved Him best, to whom He had returned and shown something of the

Risen Life, at last saw Him snatched away; 'a cloud received Him out of their sight.' You would think it was a very bitter moment: when all they loved and depended on left them and they were placed in an apparent loneliness. And all that St. Luke says about that is 'they worshipped Him and returned to Jerusalem with great joy!' Without their Master and in great joy! Can we reach *this* in our prayer?

The New Testament is full of this joyful and selfless praise. 'My spirit hath rejoiced in God my Saviour.' Objective, unearthly delight in God's action and the privilege of being caught up into God's action whatever the cost may be. 'He that is mighty hath magnified me'—real joy is all about God and real peace is all about God. They are not attributes of a cosy religion. They mean our total loving acceptance of the deep action of God through and beyond our small lives—'not doing thine own ways, nor finding thine own pleasure, nor speaking thine own words: then shalt thou delight thyself in the Lord,' says Isaiah.

Translated into our own terms that means that joy and peace and the reward of self-oblivion, dropping all considerations of the holes in our stockings, the imperfection of our characters, the poverty of our prayers, the uselessness of our lives and giving ourselves with heart and mind to adoring delight in the Beauty of God. Have you not known such moments in life, when perhaps the sudden sight of a wild cherry in blossom, the abrupt disclosure of a great mountain, or the crowning moment of a great concerto, has revealed the perfect and flooded you with tranquil joy, while the fact that you are rather a sweep simply ceased to matter at all? That is a fruit of the Spirit—and the proof that it is indeed of the Spirit is this: that it is an experience that does not grow old. Even when the body is ninety-five, the saint's spirit will still be able to rejoice in the Lord, 'singing to Father, Son and Holy Ghost. Alleluia!' Spiritual joy is a form of love: selfless delight in the Beauty of God, the Action of God, the Being of God, for and in Himself alone. It bears all things, believes all things, seeks not its own. 'Bless the Lord, O my soul! and all that is within me, bless His Holy Name!'

Joy and peace come into our lives then, when we mind more about God than we do about ourselves, when we realize what the things that matter really are; the Spirit clears up our problems about what we want or ought to be at, simplifies us and throws us back again and again on the deep and peaceful action of God. Then, whether He speeds us up or slows us down, accepts our notions or sets them aside, gives us what we want or takes it away, gives us a useful job of work or puts us on the shelf—that serenity which is a fruit of the Spirit, a sign of God's secret support, does not fail us.

WAITING UPON GOD

We have seen how the expanding creative life of God in our soul, if we give it space, will produce as its first-fruits, at the very centre of our being where the innermost self responds to God, a steady, self-oblivious gladness and a profound tranquillity. Those are the characteristics of a life of communion with God: the joy and peace of a soul adhering to Him, a joy and peace perhaps specially felt in their deep mystery and reality in times of suffering, when the spirit transforms the natural rebellion of body and mind into acceptance of frustration and pain. Nothing is more marked in the lives of the Saints than this. And how much we need that established temperature of God-given peace and joy, that climate of Eternity, at our centre, if we are to keep our feet in these unsteady times, for on the outer edge the conditions are very different. There we are always exposed to low pressure systems developing over Central Europe and small local disturbances too. How is the Spirit that indwells us to affect our responses there?

The next fruit of the Spirit, says St Paul, is long-suffering and gentleness—much patient endurance as regards what life does to us, much loving-kindness, care, consideration in all contacts with other lives. Here another region is submitted to God's influence and in consequence another source of strain taken away. If the first three fruits form a little group growing up at the soul's very centre, gentleness and long-suffering are borne on the branches that stretch out towards the world. They are the earnest of what Ruysbroeck calls the widespreading nature of love, giving itself to all in common, kind to the unjust as well as the just.

Consider first the long-suffering of God, the long-suffering and gentleness of Absolute Perfection and Absolute Power, and how the further we press into the deeps of spiritual experience, the more those qualities are seen.

How God looks past the imperfections of men (as we look past those of children), with what unexacting love He accepts and uses the faulty. See how Christ deliberately chooses Peter; while completely realizing Peter, his unreliable qualities, his boasting and cocksureness, his prompt capitulation to fear. Peter's family must have thought, 'Thank Heaven! a chance for the tiresome creature now' when he joined the Apostolic band. But Christ did not just put up with him. He offered him a continual and special friendship, knowing what was in the man. He took Peter into the inner fastness of Gethsemane and asked for his prayer and did not get it. (Is that the way we handle our tiresome and unreliable friends? Because it is with personal contacts we have always got to begin.) It was to Peter Christ addressed His rare reproach, 'What! Could you not watch one hour?' and it was from this that Peter went to the denial. Yet in spite of all, the long-suffering love and trust of Christ won in the end and made Peter the chief of the Apostles—the Rock—what irony!—on which He built the Church. He was right, for here the Church is now. In Peter's care and to Peter's love Christ left the feeding of the sheep: a remarkable sequel. Who shines in that series of events? Christ or Peter? Christ shines—but Peter is transformed. Christ's attitude and action are only possible to holiness and they are justified by results. Here is a standard set for us in our dealings with the faulty. The fruit of the Spirit is never rigorism but always long-suffering. No startling high standard. No all or nothing demands. But gentleness and tolerance in spiritual, moral, emotional, intellectual judgements and claims. No hurry and no exactingness. That is not easy when we are keen, and see the work we love imperilled by someone else's fault. But God, says St. Paul, is a God of patience. He works in tranquillity and tranquillity seldom goes into partnership with speed. God breaks few records but He always arrives in the end. One of the best things we can do for souls is to wait and one of the worst things is to force the issue. God lets the plant grow at its own pace. That is why He can bring forth supernatural beauty in and through imperfect instruments.

All of us need this grace of long-suffering in respect of our own life of prayer. There, too, we must learn to wait, realizing the degree in which it depends on God's quiet, creative action, the profound nature of the changes it demands in our whole being. We have got to become a 'new creature,' as the New Testament says, a creature living towards God. If it takes nine months to make a natural baby, would it be very surprising if it took nine years to make a supernatural baby? Tarry thou the Lord's leisure. . . .

DOING OUR DUTY

Goodness and Faithfulness—we think of them as the supreme virtues of the plain man. Yet they too are the fruit of the Spirit. In the long run we cannot really manage them without God. The good citizen, good employer, good artist, good worker—the faithful husband or wife or mother—in these, too, Divine Love, selfless charity, is bringing forth its fruits within the natural order and on the natural scale: proclaiming the dignity and possibilities of our human life on all levels, disclosing the full meaning of the Word made Flesh. Another lesson in not being highminded; another invitation to come off our self-chosen spiritual perch, whatever it may be, and face the facts of human life.

Faithfulness is consecration in overalls. It is the steady acceptance and performance of the common duty and immediate task without any reference to personal preferences—because it is there to be done and so is a manifestation of the Will of God. It is Elizabeth Leseur settling down each day to do the household accounts quite perfectly (when she would much rather have been in church) and saying 'the duties of my station come before everything else.' It is Brother Lawrence taking his turn in the kitchen, and St. Francis de Sales taking the burden of a difficult diocese and saying, 'I have now little time for prayer—but I do what is the same.'

The fruits of the Spirit get less and less showy as we go on. Faithfulness means continuing quietly with the job we have been given, in the situation where we have been placed; not yielding to the restless desire for change. It means tending the lamp quietly for God without wondering how much longer it has got to go on. Steady, unsensational driving, taking good care of the car. A lot of the road to heaven has to be taken at thirty miles per hour. It means keeping everything in your charge in good order for love's sake, rubbing up the silver, polishing the glass even though you know the Master will not be looking round the pantry next weekend. If your life is really part of the apparatus of the Spirit, that is the sort of life it must be. You have got to be the sort of cat who can be left alone with the canary: the sort of dog who follows, hungry and thirsty but tail up, to the very end of the day.

Faithfulness and Goodness—they *are* doggy qualities. Fancy that as a Fruit of the Spirit! But then the Spirit is Love, and doggy love is a very good sort of love, humble, selfless and enduring. Faithfulness is the quality of the friend, refusing no test and no trouble, loyal, persevering; not at the mercy of emotional ups and downs or getting tired when things are tiresome. In the interior life of prayer faithfulness points steadily to God and His purposes, away from self and its preoccupations, specially spiritual preoccupations. It was a very faithful soul who said, 'We ought simply to hate thinking of our own spiritual lives.' You cannot imagine a nice retriever fussing about his own inner state, carefully inspecting his sins, or worrying about whether he is being directed quite right. He just trusts his master and his own sense of smell and carries on.

The indwelling Spirit of God is never a source of trouble and scruple, but a stabilizing power, a constant. 'When I go up to Heaven Thou are there; when I go down into Sheol, Thou art there also'—when I am exultant and when I am depressed. Light and dark to Thee are both alike! The friendship of God is like that, and He asks the same faithfulness from us in return. It takes a brave and loving soul to understand and respond to this sturdy faithfulness of God, for there is nothing sentimental about it. 'Thou of very faithfulness hast caused me to be troubled,' says the Psalmist (Psalm 119.v 75). The faithful father and teacher does what is needed, not what is nice. He will even risk losing the child's affection rather than fail the child's real needs—giving stern tests when tests are needed, withdrawing apparent support that courage and initiative may be learned, giving the distasteful duty, withdrawing the dangerous joy; bit by bit producing in the soul a fidelity that shall answer His own.

The Fruits of the Spirit: Evelyn Underhill

Surely we may say that the chief struggle of the Passion, the awful crisis of Gethsemane, was a struggle in which we are shown the supreme heights of faithfulness, a struggle for strength to see it through to the end, whatever the cost. 'Let this cup depart . . . nevertheless not my will but Thine be done!'

The first step taken towards Calvary was the worst: but in the first step all was achieved. Be thou faithful unto death—and I will give thee the Crown of Life. Faithfulness is one of the sturdy qualities most dear to the heart of God. Peter was offered just the same chance of the same royal virtue. Jesus was victorious on the Cross. Peter was defeated, warming himself by the fire for the night was cold. I wonder how *we* should act if the same sort of crisis, charged with fear and quite devoid of consolation, came our way? It is a crisis which in some form all the saints have had to face.'

THE TEST OF FAITHFULNESS

Now let us consider three of Our Lord's great lessons upon faithfulness gathered together in Matthew 25. Here are three examples of faithfulness of the difficult kind that is exercised, not towards God when we feel him present, but to God when He seems to be absent. And these lessons show it to be a stalwart sort of virtue making great demands on us, having little connection with feeling, and not achieved without deliberate, continuous, costly effort of heart, mind and will.

First comes the story of the ten Virgins. The really faithful will have to be prudent and careful as well as devoted. We have to carry on all night; it is a long job subject to temptations of weariness and inconstancy, so we make our plans accordingly. The truly faithful take the situation seriously remembering that the ardent lamp depends on the homely oil; they do not leave it all to chance and say it will be 'all right on the night.' They take reasonable precautions—enough oil in the lamp, the rule of life, the necessary spiritual nourishment, the quiet devotional practice— to keep light going in the long night. And then the cry at dawn; and those who were faithful and prudent find the lamp of adoration is still alight.

Secondly comes the story of the Ten Talents. Faithfulness always seeks the interests of God and uses all its ability for Him with courage and skill. That often involves risks and choices and demands which seem beyond our capacity—the faithfulness of the small creature doing a hard job in the teeth of overwhelming circumstances because this is the Master's will; forgetting all about Safety First.

The third lesson is perhaps the deepest and the most searching. Faithfulness in responding to the here and now demands of men on our love and pity and service; going on and on with that loving service even although we have no sense of God; on and on with the work and the effort entailed in the feeding and clothing of the needy, the visiting of the sick—just out of loving compassion and without any glow of religious joy. That bit comes home to some of us very specially. When saw we Thee, Lord? We are to serve Him wherever He is; that is, wherever need appeals and love and compassion are awakened by its voice. Though we cannot realize it, the King is *there*—not in His beauty, but moving disguised among His people by night.

This is the faithfulness of the man who found a Treasure hid in a field. What was the Treasure? People give it various names—it was God reaching out to him, calling him—his chance of the consecrated life. When we have found the Treasure, our response must be total and faithful: the response the rich young man did not make. Sometimes it seems to us a goodly Pearl, then it is an easy problem. You see the dedicated life in its radiant beauty and though the price is very high you have no serious doubts; you buy that Pearl.

But the treasure hid in the field is a much

less attractive proposition. It is the field we have to buy, by the sacrifice of all that we have: for without the field we have no access to the treasure. It always comes to us allied with particular material circumstances and we must accept these circumstances if we want it. There is nothing attractive about the field—probably a poor bit of ground, producing a few rows of unhappy cabbages, a dump of tins and broken pots in one corner; a nasty place to dig in. Yet that is where your treasure is—the call of God to you—and it is only by paying for the field and working in the field that you are going to find it.

A moment comes in many lives when after years spent, as you feel quite properly, in cultivating your own garden, using your talents, doing very well with your special type of plant, you may be suddenly faced by the field. Rough and unattractive, yet it is made plain as the place where your treasure is. That is the time to test your faithfulness. The career sacrificed, the tastes you cannot gratify any more, the utterly uncongenial duty embraced and all else given up for it, the trying person you must take into your life, the loss of health you must cheerfully and willingly embrace, the unattractive future you must yet make fruitful for God. The only thing that matters for Christians, says St. Paul—and certainly he was called to it—is Faithfulness, working through Love. That is the very heart of the supernatural life as lived by man: turning the will towards God and keeping it turned. Faithfulness working through love accepts the field, however unattractive, and accepts it, not for its own sake but for God. To refuse or avoid it is to break the ordained sequence of graces by which God is leading you to Himself, to check the development of the fruit of His Spirit in your soul.

Whatever path we have to travel, in whatever department we are asked to serve, we soon realize that sturdy faithfulness alone will see us through and that long fidelity up hill and down dale, in sickness and health, in riches and poverty, in good weather and bad, is not going to be very easy to maintain. Of ourselves we cannot do it. It needs the abiding presence of love, joy and peace at the centre of our being and a continuous effort towards long-suffering and gentleness. In fact we shall only maintain it in so far as we do it with and for God. But if we do maintain it, that will suffice. Nothing more striking is required. Well done thou good and faithful servant. Christ thought that said everything; set His mark of entire approval on a life. Not—Well done my holy little choir-boy singing that high note like a cherub—but—Well done, my trusty, worthy, solid, responsible servant, whom I can leave in charge of the animals and know they will not be forgotten, or to whom I can give my treasure to lay out and know it will be properly spent.

'THE BOTTOM OF THE STAIRS'

'Though I give my body to be burned,' said St. Paul, 'and have not love, I am nothing.' I do not as a supernatural being exist. And now he gives us another and much more surprising test of spiritual vitality. Though you feel an unconquerable love, joy and peace, though you are gentle, long-suffering, good in all your personal relationships, though you are utterly faithful in your service of God— in the end of the only proof that all this is truly fruit of the Spirit, Christ in you and not just your own idea, is the presence of the last two berries on the bunch: not showy berries, not prominently placed, but absolutely decisive for the classification of the plant. Meekness and Temperance, says the Authorized Version, or, as we may quite properly translate, Humility and Moderation. That means our possession of the crowning grace of creatureliness: knowing our own size and own place, the self-oblivion and quietness with which we fit into God's great scheme instead of having a jolly little scheme of our own, and are content to bring forth the fruit of His Spirit, according to our own measure, here and now in space and time.

Humility and Moderation—the graces of the self-forgetful soul—we might almost expect that if we have grasped all that the Incarnation really means—God and His love, manifest not in some peculiar and supernatural spiritual manner, but in ordinary human nature. Christ, first-born of many brethren, content to be one of us, living the family life, and from within His Church inviting the souls of men to share His family life. In the family circle there is room for the childish and the imperfect and the naughty, but the uppish is always out of place.

We have got down to the bottom of the stairs now and are fairly sitting on the mat. But the proof that it is the right flight and leads up to the Divine Charity, is the radiance that pours down from the upper storey: the joy and peace in which the whole is bathed and which floods our whole being here in the lowest place. How right St Paul was to put these two fruits at the end of his list, for as a rule they are the very last we acquire. At first we simply do not see the point. But the saints have always seen it. When Angela of Foligno was dying, her disciples asked for a last message and she, who had been called a Mistress in Theology and whose Visions of the Being of God are among the greatest the medieval mystics have left us, had only one thing to say to them as her farewell: 'Make yourselves small! Make yourselves very small.'

The approach to God is the approach to Reality and the grace of His Spirit in us is the grace of that Wisdom whereby we can begin to know a little of Reality. The result of this can only be to make us feel very small, indeed smaller as our vision clears. In Revelation it is the saints and elders nearest God who cast down their crowns when they adore Him.

The lesser fry, further off, are quite content to go on wearing theirs.

We have been thinking of the fruits brought forth in our souls by the Holy Creative Spirit of God. In this world that Holy Spirit is known to us as the Spirit of Christ. In Him it was made manifest. He discloses its very nature in human terms. He gives it to His Church and it shines again in His Saints. But that same Spirit is also the Spirit of the Eternal Wisdom, the Spirit which broods over creation, which is the Lord and Giver of Life. This is what we mean when we say that Christ is the Fullness of all things, in Him they are gathered up and revealed to men. Through our Lord's self-giving we are enabled to reach out through Him and His human life to His life in the Blessed Sacrament and at last to the mystery of the direct action on our souls of the Creative Will of God. Is not that enough to make us feel very small?

All the saving acts of the Passion, when we consider that the One who did them was the

Eternal Word made flesh, were acts of humiliation—the acts of one who had come down to the bottom of the stairs—'Having loved His own, He loved them to the end'—by an act of humble service and love, not an exercise of beneficent power. Friedrich von Hugel said that he could never read without deep emotion, the story of Christ the Holy, meekly washing and drying the feet of that poor little collection of coward followers. Yet perhaps this very remembrance was one of the things which helped to turn those followers into saints. So too in Gethsemane perhaps the final anguish was the discovery in One totally devoted to the Father that, sharing our human weakness, He could not face without flinching, all this devotedness had to involve. And again on the Via Dolorosa He had to accept the physical weakness which made Him unable to bear His own Cross. These are parts of the pattern put before us. Think of them.

Christ never suggests that it is necessarily the most efficient, intelligent or fully devel-

oped person who is most fit for eternal life,
or most pleasing to God—that is one of the
most foolish illusions of the natural man. His
thoughts are not our thoughts; nor His values
our values. It is far better, says Christ, to go
lame and blind into heaven than to be very
capable and clear-sighted and sure of yourself,
to make others stumble, and end on the rub-
bish heap. The only thing that counts, and
proves the presence of Divine Life in us, is
total dedication to God, total dependence on
Him. The small, helpless child at the font
with new life in it, not the successful preacher
in the pulpit, is the typical Christian; the last
shall be the first, and the first last.

SAYING 'YES' TO GOD

Humility and moderation at the heart of our
prayer quiet the soul and protect us against
the spiritual itch. 'It sometimes comes into
my head,' says De Caussade, 'to wonder
whether I have ever properly confessed my

sins, whether God has ever forgiven me my
sins, whether I am in a good or bad spiritual
state. What progress have I made in prayer or
the interior life? When this happens I say to
myself at once, God has chosen to hide all
this from me, so that I may just blindly aban-
don myself to His mercy. So I submit myself
and I adore His decision . . . . He is the Master: may all that He wills be accomplished in
me; I want no grace, no merit, no perfection
but that which shall please Him. His will
alone is sufficient for me and that will always
be the measure of my desires.' Meekness and
temperance taught out of his own experience
by a very great master of the spiritual life. In
your soul's life towards God, then, that humble moderation has, or should have, an important place and many special applications.
It is far better to realize a few truths, produce
a few acts of worship, but do them *well*, leav-
ing to others those truths and those practices
which for you are dark or involve strain. Do
not entertain the notion that you ought to

advance in your prayer. If you do, you will only find you have put on the brake instead of the accelerator. All real progress in spiritual things comes gently, imperceptibly, and is the work of God. Our crude efforts spoil it. Know yourself for the childish, limited and dependent soul you are. Remember that the only growth which matters happens without our knowledge and that trying to stretch ourselves is both dangerous and silly. Think of the Infinite Goodness, never of your own state. Realize that the very capacity to pray at all is the free gift of the Divine Love and be content with St. Francis de Sales' favourite prayer, in which all personal religion is summed up: 'Yes, Father! Yes! and always Yes!'

That puts things in their right order and makes us realize again that it is God that matters, not the elaborate furniture of the sanctuary where you meet. And as a matter of fact, His taste in furniture is simple. He is better suited by a few good pieces the right size for your little room than by a litter of theological and devotional ornaments. The limits within which each of us can realize and respond to Him are well-defined. Do not try to elude those limits or achieve something you have read about; it merely means your prayers will get puffy and out of shape. Let us rejoice in the great adoring acts and splendid heroisms of God's great lovers and humbly do the little bit we can. We too have our place.

If all the greasers and plate-layers had wanted to drive the engine the 9.15 would never have arrived. Many humble vocations faithfully accepted contributed to that. It was the work of the whole body of many members, having gifts differing according to the Grace that was given them. And Grace is God Himself, His loving energy at work within His Church and within our souls—and that is what matters.

Looking back on these meditations we begin perhaps to see a new unity in them. The bringing forth in our souls of the fruit of the

The Fruits of the Spirit: Evelyn Underhill

Spirit is realized now as one single indivisible act of the Divine Love; God, the Spirit of Spirits, indwelling His creature and moulding it to the pattern of Christ. Just as a seed cast into the ground has hidden within it the whole character of the plant that is to be, in its form, colour, beauty, fragrance—and nothing we can do can change that character, though we may check its development if we will: so the seed of Divine Charity, received into the ground of the soul, will grow true to type if we let it, and bring forth its spiritual fruits. And this growth arises from, and depends upon, the presence in the soul's deeps of the Abiding and the Perfect—the Love and Joy and Peace of the Eternal God.

Only because in her prayer she can again and again resort to that ground of her being, where beyond Time she breathes the quiet air of the supernatural life, can the spiritual seed grow, thrive and produce within time the homely and precious fruits of long-suffering and gentleness, of goodness and faithfulness, of meekness and temperance—qualities which are called forth and tested by the very character of the world of succession in which we are placed by God and required to grow up to the stature of Christ. There, in those deeps, the seed germinates, the roots plunge down into the Eternal, ever more deeply with the simplification and self-abandonment of our prayer; and from those deeps the sap of the spirit rises and the strong plant grows and feeds.

Here, in all the tensions, contacts and opportunities of our everyday experience, the small, commonplace circumstances of our life, whose spiritual value we so easily underestimate, its fruits are brought forth and matured.

THE COMING OF THE LORD

At the beginning of her course the Church looks out towards Eternity, and realizes her own poverty and imperfection and her utter dependence on this perpetual coming of God.

The Fruits of the Spirit: Evelyn Underhill

Advent is, of course, first of all a preparation for Christmas; which commemorates God's saving entrance into history in the Incarnation of Jesus Christ.

Whilst all things were in quiet silence and night was in the midst of her swift course: thine Almighty Word leapt down from heaven out of thy royal throne. Alleluia.

A tremendous spiritual event then took place; something which disclosed the very nature of God and His relation to His universe. But there was little to show for it on the surface of life. All men saw was a poor girl unconditionally submitted to God's Will, and a baby born in difficult circumstances. And this contrast between the outward appearance and the inner reality is true of all the comings of God to us. We must be very loving and very alert if we want to recognize them in their earthly disguise. Again and again He comes and the revelation is not a bit what we expect.

So the next lesson Advent should teach us is that our attitude towards Him should always be one of humble eager expectancy. Our spiritual life depends on His perpetual coming to us, far more than on our going to Him. Every time a channel is made for Him He comes; every time our hearts are open to Him He enters, bringing a fresh gift of His very life, and on that life we depend. We should think of the whole power and splendour of God as always pressing in upon our small souls. 'In Him we live and move and have our being.' But that power and splendour mostly reach us in homely and inconspicuous ways; in the sacraments, and in our prayers, joys and sorrows and in all opportunities of loving service. This means that one of the most important things in our prayer is the eagerness and confidence with which we throw ourselves open to His perpetual coming. There should always be more waiting than striving in a Christian's prayer—an absolute dependence on the self-giving charity of God. 'As dew shall our God descend on us.'

As we draw near Christmas, this sense of our own need and of the whole world's need of God's coming—never greater perhaps than it is now—becomes more intense. In the great Advent Antiphons which are said in the week before Christmas we seem to hear the voice of the whole suffering creation saying 'Come! give us wisdom, give us light, deliver us, liberate us, lead us, teach us how to live. Save us.' And we, joining in that prayer, unite our need with the one need of the whole world. We have to remember that the answer to the prayer was not a new and wonderful world order but Bethlehem and the Cross; a life of complete surrender to God's Will; and we must expect this answer to be worked out in our own lives in terms of humility and sacrifice.

If our lives are ruled by this spirit of Advent, this loving expectation of God, they will have a quality quite difference from that of conventional piety. For they will be centred on an entire and conscious dependence upon the supernatural love which supports us; hence all self-confidence will be destroyed in them and replaced by perfect confidence in God. They will be docile to His pressure, and obedient to every indication of His Will.

THE DEMANDS OF CHRIST

Our Lord demanded great renunciation of those who wanted to follow Him. He never suggested that the Christian life was an easy or comfortable affair. The substance of what He asked is summed up in what are called the 'evangelical counsels'—Poverty, Chastity and Obedience. We know that those who enter religious communities accept these counsels in their most literal form. They do give up all their possessions, their natural and human relationships, the freedom of their wills. But in one way or another, something of their spirit is needed by everyone who really desires to follow Christ. The New Testament means what it says when it demands poverty of spirit, purity of heart and filial obedience from all who would do this. And the reason is, that each of these qualities in a different way detaches us from the unreal and self-regarding interests with which (almost without knowing it) we usually fill up our lives. They simplify us, clear the ground for God; so that our relation of utter dependence on Him stands out as the one reality of our existence. So it might be profitable for us this Lent to meditate on the three Counsels and see what light they cast on our own lives.

First, think of *Poverty.* Even outward Poverty, a hard and simple life, the dropping for love's sake of the many things we feel we 'must have' is a great help in the way of the Spirit. Far more precious is that inward Poverty of which it is the sacrament; which frees us from possessions and possessiveness and does away with the clutch of 'the I, the Me and the Mine' upon our souls. We can all strive for this internal grace, this attitude of soul, and it is a very important part of the life of prayer. The Holy Spirit is called the Giver of Gifts and the Father of the Poor; but His cherishing action is only really felt by those who acknowledge their own deep poverty— who realize that we have literally nothing of our own, but are totally dependent on God and on that natural world in which God has placed us and which is the sacramental vehicle of His action. When we grasp this we are ready to receive His gifts.

Chastity. The Counsel of Chastity does not, of course, mean giving up marriage but something much more subtle and penetrating. It really means the spirit of poverty applied to our emotional life—all the clutch and feverishness of desire, the 'I want' and 'I must have' taken away and replaced by absolute single-mindedness, purity of heart. This may involve a deliberate rationing of the time and energy we give to absorbing personal relationships with others—unnecessary meetings,

talks and letters—to special tastes and interests, or, worst of all, self-occupied daydreams
and broodings about ourselves, cravings for
sympathy and interest.

Obedience. This means the total surrender
of our wills, which are the great obstacles to
our real self-giving to God. The more we get
rid of self-chosen aims, however good, the
more supple we are to His pressure, the nearer
we get to the pattern of the Christian life
which is summed up in 'not my will but Thine
be done.' Then, not before, we are ready to
be used as God's tools and contribute to His
purpose. Since God is the true doer of all that
is done, it is always for Him to initiate and
for us to respond, and this willing response
is the essence of obedience. Obedience means
more freedom not less, for it lifts the burden
of perpetual choice, and in so doing actually
increases our power of effective action by
making us the instruments of God's unlimited
action. When the whole Church is thus obedient to Him it will be what it is meant to be,

'a fellowship of creative heaven-led souls' with power to fulfil its vocation of transforming the world. There is an obligation laid on each of us to do our best to contribute to this great end, and ready obedience to the human beings among whom He has placed us is a very good way of learning obedience to God.

THE POWER OF THE SPIRIT
(A letter)

Dear Member of the Prayer Group,

From talks which I have had with some of you lately, and letters that I have received, I gather that the keeping of our rule of prayer and especially the sort of life and outlook which ought to go with the prayer does not get easier as time goes on. Most of you are very busy and often too tired or anxious to clear the space which is needed for concentration on God's worship. Practical life presses more and more hardly. Strain is increasing. We are all more and more conscious of the uncertainties of our time. Not everyone can face the results of an air raid with an unshaken belief in the goodness of the universe and the loving-kindness of God. Institutional religion too often seems stiff, disappointing, remote from actuality in contrast to the awful realities of evil, danger, suffering, death among which we live. Many of you cannot any longer find time for the regular theological reading which was a chief intellectual interest and support, and gave as it were a background to your religion. But all these various obstacles and difficulties are simply part of the circumstances, in which God requires us to serve Him: and we shall deal with them best if we look at them from this point of view. They are there to be used; and should brace not baffle us, help not hinder us. No Christian escapes a taste of the wilderness on the way to the Promised Land; and the wilderness confronts this generation in a very harsh and concrete form. Often it may compel us to dwell for a long time in a mental or a devotional desert, where religion seems dry and tasteless, and we find very little intellectual or devotional food. This is all part of our training, and helps us, in a disagreeable way, to realize our entire dependence on God. We shall learn its lessons best if we make a real effort when things are most difficult to keep a firm hold on 'the great centralities of religion' as Baron von Hugel loved to call them—the tremendous facts which lie behind all our practice—and try to realize a little more fully the deep truths which they reveal. If we do this faithfully, as and where we can, we shall find that God will secretly feed our souls through these channels; and we shall return to the intellectual study of theology or the fuller and more fervent practice of religion, when the time comes for it, with an entirely new understanding of the meaning and unfathomable depths of its great truths.

For God, Christ, the Church, the earthly life and death of Jesus, are not academic propositions, but spiritual facts. We do not learn

their true meaning by reading books about
them or discussing them but by dwelling upon
them in a spirit of prayer: and there is no
sphere of work, however hard, monotonous
or homely, in which it is impossible ever to
do that. The little story of St. Thomas Aqui-
nas putting away his ink horn and his pen,
saying 'I have seen too much, I can write no
more!' tells us more about the spiritual fact of
religion, that is to say the communion of our
souls with the Mystery that surrounds us,
than does the whole of his great *Summa Theo-
logica*. A fact is not a notion about reality; it
is a living part of the reality in which God has
placed us; and as we look at it humbly and
steadily it will unfold and disclose to us more
and more of the truth it contains.

I am writing to you at the moment in the
Christian year when, as it were, we pause and
look back on the richest cluster of such spiritual facts ever revealed to man. Paschal Time,
to give its old name to the interval between
Easter and Ascension, marks the end of the

historical manifestation of the Word Incarnate, and the beginning of His hidden life within the Church. But the quality of that hidden life, in which as members of the Body of Christ we are all required to take part, is the quality which the historic life revealed. From the very beginning the Church has been sure that the series of events which were worked out to their inevitable end in Holy Week sum up and express the deepest secrets of the relation of God to men.

That means, of course, that Christianity can never be merely a pleasant or consoling religion. It is a stern business. It is concerned with the salvation through sacrifice and love of a world in which, as we can all see now, evil and cruelty are rampant. Its supreme symbol is the Crucifix—the total and loving self-giving of man to the redeeming purposes of God.

Because we are all the children of God we all have our part to play in His redemptive plan; and the Church consists of those loving souls who have accepted this obligation, with all that it costs. Its members are all required to live, each in their own way, through the sufferings and self-abandonment of the Cross; as the only real contribution which they can make to the redemption of the world. Christians, like their Master, must be ready to accept the worst that evil and cruelty can do to them, and vanquish it by the power of love.

For if sacrifice, total self-giving to God's mysterious purpose, is what is asked of us, His answer to that sacrifice is the gift of power. Easter and Whitsuntide complete the Christian Mystery by showing us first Our Lord Himself and then his chosen apostles possessed of a new power—the power of the Spirit—which changed every situation in which they were placed. That supernatural power is still the inheritance of every Christian, and our idea of Christianity is distorted and incomplete unless we rely on it. It is this power and only this which can bring in the new Christian society of which we hear so much. We ought to pray for it; expect it and trust it; and as we do this, we shall gradually become more and more sure of it.